LIGHT
WORKER

A CALL TO AUTHENTICITY
— • —
LLOYD MATTHEW THOMPSON

STARFIELD

Starfield Press
Oklahoma City, OK

LIGHTWORKER: A CALL TO AUTHENTICITY
by Lloyd Matthew Thompson
Copyright © 2013 Starfield Press - All Rights Reserved

First printing 2013
Second printing 2020

Paperback ISBN: 978-0615873565

Starfield Press
www.StarfieldPress.com
Oklahoma City, OK

Akasha Shore
www.AkashaShore.com

DISCLAIMER: The information in this book does not substitute for medical care. Do not discontinue use of medication, or disregard the advice of your medical professional. This information is a supplement to any current health care treatment, and is not intended to diagnose or cure. Always consult your doctor. The author and publisher of this book are not responsible for the actions of the reader.

Cover design by Lloyd Matthew Thompson

LIGHTWORKER
A CALL TO AUTHENTICITY

— • —

LLOYD MATTHEW THOMPSON

CONTENTS

FOREWORD 11
INTRODUCTION 17

PART I — THE LIGHT PART
1 • THE WORD..25
2 • THE BURN..31
3 • THE FLUFF...41
4 • THE POWER...47
5 • THE DARK...57
6 • THE LIGHT 65

PART II — THE WORKER PART
7 • THE SHOCK 75
8 • THE WORK...83
9 • THE FEAR 91
10 • THE GAME 99
11 • THE AUTHENTICITY 107

ABOUT THE AUTHOR...................................119

To all who have helped me to this place,
by kicking and clashing,
or loving and guiding —
every method
in every instance
was exactly what I needed.

Thank you.

FOREWORD

WHEN I WAS ASKED to write the foreword for *Lightworker: A Call to Authenticity*, the honor humbled me in several ways.

There are experiences and lessons brought to us that allow us to learn and to create our own clearer path to finding our Authentic Self. Lloyd has personally helped me along this part of my Journey here on the Earthly plane at this time of stepping into my Lightworker (Authentic Self) role, not only through his healing energy work, friendship, and support, but also through his writings.

Whether you are new to your Lightworking role, or are a veteran in these areas, it is important at this time on Planet Earth that we practice what we preach to the best of our ability, showing love and compassion in our daily interactions.

In *Lightworker*, Lloyd challenges us to allow

ourselves to take a deeper look inside ourselves, to remove the debris that clouds our being, and to explore and step into our Authentic Self.

Lightworker is written simply, from the Heart, and touches upon fears that all Lightworkers encounter at one time or another.

Lloyd also shares some of his own experiences that have led him to step more fully into his own Authentic Self, and exactly what that means to him. Who better to write this book but someone who walks their talk on a daily basis?

When I agreed to write this foreword, it gave me an opportunity to step just a bit further into exploring more of my own Authentic Self as a writer. Was I nervous? Yes. But after going inward, I took a leap of faith, and found I was actually excited to explore this part of my being.

Our planet is aching for Oneness, healing, and Unity. Through love, and the expression of our Authentic Self, we heal as a Whole.

It is my hope that after you read *Lightworker*, you feel this calling in your Heart, and give yourself permission to be Authentic You.

Tamara Lynn Rectenwald, CCH
www.TamaraRectenwald.com

LIGHTWORKER

A CALL TO AUTHENTICITY

— • —

LLOYD MATTHEW THOMPSON

INTRODUCTION

THE KEY TO YOUR success is your authenticity.

There.

I said it.

There is now no further need to continue writing this book, because that is the sum and the whole of it all.

But your inner Heart has led you to pick up a book with such a title as *Lightworker: A Call to Authenticity* for a reason, hasn't it?

Perhaps I should continue then…

LET ME FIRST BEGIN by stating I did not intend to write this book. I had just finished *The Galaxy Healer's Guide*, and was very much looking forward to focusing fully on my fictional stories for a while — although *they* always insist on portraying truths and lessons as well.

I had had my fill of teaching and leading for a while, having recently passed the reins on organizing and running the local metaphysical fairs, and wanted to lose myself for a time in the worlds of my mind... or at least until I finished *The Energy Anthology* series.

But I have always been an Observer, a Listener. From the time I was a child, I've always been quiet, and kept to myself, yet watched all around with alertness and mindfulness. I've always had a sort of natural meter, alerting me if something is "right on," "touching right on, yet still a bit *off*," or flat-out "off." Growing up in the church was probably the best place I could have been to polish this intuition.

And the more I observe, especially in these times, the more my Heart breaks.

In every circle and every culture, I see hollow and misunderstood actions performed without personal thought. I see "spiritual" groups operated as masks for sheer ego or the manipulation and control of others. I see spirituality posed and projected by people both as a crutch to avoid responsibility, and as an excuse for not confronting their own shadows, which is a *huge* requirement for true growth.

I've gotten into the habit of keeping lists of comments and ideas as they occur to me, and in the summer of 2012, I began a list I had labeled

What I See Wrong. I thought this was simply a list of ideas to draw from when writing various blogs and articles, yet this list kept jumping out to me, and would not let me rest or focus on other projects. I knew then this was meant to be compiled and expanded into a complete book — and that it was writing itself, before I ever set fingers to keyboard for it.

Side note: I realize there is not *really* any such thing as "right" and "wrong" — there is only the most *helpful* for all involved, as opposed to the most *harmful* for all involved. That list would have been better labeled *What Is Not Beneficial for the Growth and Evolution/Enlightenment of The People, The Planet, and The Universe...* but that would probably have been too long to fit in my Gmail task list app.

And so, the key to your success is your authenticity.

The key to your *growth.*

Whether it is physical success or spiritual growth you are interested in, the whole of it all rests upon your authenticity.

Your *real*ness.

My intention with this book is not to preach, scold, or even condemn anyone or anything. I am nowhere near perfect in these things myself, and write them as an examination and meditation into my *own* mindsets and actions above all.

I am no teacher, prophet, or authority on anything—I am only a man, standing beside you, growing toward and dedicated to the Light of Awareness, the same as you.

My Heart and my hope here is to merely inspire thought, introspection, and self-examination. That is all that is needed to set the momentum of change and authenticity rolling.

If you are honestly and truthfully doing your absolute best, for yourself and this world around you, then *you* are a Lightworker.

— PART I —

THE **LIGHT** PART

WORDS ARE FUNNY THINGS. They are able to hold multiple layers of meanings, evolve to mean the *opposite* of their original meaning, or even completely *lose* any solid meaning at all. Misuse, misunderstandings, and misconceptions add even more confusion to the lexicons and dictionaries.

Words are merely symbols created to communicate thought, and can be changed, interchanged, or disregarded — yet their *energy* bears the same weight and intention nevertheless.

A rock is always a rock, even if it is called a *mwamba* in a foreign land. It still is what it is. But the word *rock* has also come to mean "*to accomplish something well*," as in "You rock that task!" Another definition of it can be "*something amazing*," as in "That rocks!"

The latter definition happens to be a current

replacement for the term *"cool"* — which also means *"something amazing"* in that frame of reference. *Cool* lost much of its power over time and use, and eventually a new term to communicate to another how amazing something is naturally came into use. Many societies have sacred words that are forbidden to be spoken for this very reason.

Lightworker is a term that is fast approaching this stage of overuse.

So many in the spiritual and metaphysical communities toss this word around so casually, claiming its title for themselves as if it proves the Universe itself has divinely and personally blessed them and placed them above all other people, and above all boundaries. They flaunt it as if it were an all-access pass to excuse anything and everything they decide to do, basis or no basis.

This sort of use is merely a title for the ego, the equivalent of honorary initials after a legal name to demonstrate importance or education. The mask of this title is projected outward for all to see, but the energy within — which cannot be masked — reveals otherwise. The two do not agree. Eventually, people's physical actions reveal their true motives, and the use of its honorable implications is shown to have been *mis*used for vain and selfish motives.

This breaks my Heart.

Can a photographer simply walk into a surgery room and say *I've decided I'm a doctor now – I will perform this operation*, and be allowed to do so? Unless they can provide documentation that they have had the necessary training and certification to do surgery, they wouldn't get farther than the scrub-in.

It seems to be growing increasingly apparent that there are many who have not truly sat with the word *Lightworker*, or meditated on what it really means. They seem to have not contemplated what it even means to *be* a Lightworker before adopting it on their business cards and websites as part of their "identity."

Whether the term used is Lightworker, Healer, Spiritual Counselor, or Priest, the energy behind the word implies that one holds the highest standards, and is dedicated to the highest good of all.

This is the authenticity that those claiming any position such as these must examine themselves against *daily*.

Of course, there are many who *do* understand the meaning and weight of Lightworker, and do not take on this title lightly (pun intended!). They strive toward the highest purpose of Lightworker night and day, selflessly giving their all. Yet even in this is risk of imbalance – if you are depleted and not in your own healthiest condition, how do you expect to be able to be of help to anyone else?

Constant mindfulness is very important in these areas of work.

What exactly *is* a Lightworker?

A Lightworker is one who is naturally dedicated to changing this reality, to shining a "light" on the truths and ultimate realities in this place, and to making a difference on this plane of existence, in whatever way they can. A Lightworker is a "placeholder," who by their very example of impeccable and honest living endeavors to demonstrate the highest vibration of life and love, and in so doing, encourage others toward their own healing of mind, body, and spirit. A Lightworker is not afraid to do what is necessary when needed, and is also not afraid to do *nothing,* when needed — and has the detached discernment to know when to do which.

All these are embedded directly into the DNA coding of a Lightworker, but all these are also a daily *choice*. Free will is one of the most important laws in this place. No one is ever forced to do anything they do not choose to do — and there is no "punishment" if we choose to not do something the Universe suggests.

Change is a key word in the role of a Lightworker, and another aspect that is glossed over in the routine of saying all the "right" things and giving all the "right" answers. We look out our windows, we see the state of this world and all the horrible things going on at this time, and we say, "Oh my! This has gotten completely out of hand! How did it come to this? This needs to change!"

But then what?

Do we realize what we're saying?

What do we truly believe *change* entails — merely twitching our noses, crossing our fingers, saying the word and making it so? Those actions may add necessary *oomph* to the work of making a difference, depending on the individual, but they are ultimately not what creates the change. Too often, we say the words without feeling or meaning them, then turn back inside our comfortable homes, our cozy boxes, forgetting the unbalanced world outside our window. Someone else will handle it. It will all get sorted out somehow.

But how?

The starting point is *you*.

Everything in this universe has a starting point, a "ground zero." Drop a pebble into a pond, and begin ripples of perfect circles from that starting point. Flash a bolt of lightning to suddenly increase the pressure and temperature of an area, and start a roll of thunder that can easily shake an entire building. Switch a light bulb on in a dark room, and start a shift of the immediate environment at the speed of 299,792,458 meters per second.

Spark an ember in the forest of this world,

and start an infectious flame that can quickly and easily spread from limb to limb.

With arms outstretched and Hearts ablaze, you are the fire that has come to purify this world. Lightworkers are the ones who have come to do the "grunt work" behind the scenes, meant to spark the flame in others, and shift the energy that much brighter.

The difference here is *you*.

On this planet, it seems as if change is resisted at all costs—and work is stubbornly avoided nearly as much. Yet the entire second half of the word Lightworker is *worker*. You must be willing to work if you want to be considered a Lightworker. This includes taking care of and watching out for yourself as well as others.

And just as Little Red Riding Hood was able to pick up clues that eventually allowed her to piece together that it was in fact not her grandmother in that bed, if your energy or actions do not match what you claim, both those who are "awake" and those who are not will know.

• 2 •
THE BURN

THE OLD PARENTING METHOD of "Do as I say, not as I do" no longer has a place in this new reality, as well as the "Because I said so" reasoning. How they ever worked at all is beyond understanding. If an authority is clearly not abiding by the rules and laws that have been set, then all motivation to obey or submit is out the window. As more people "awaken," consistency and authenticity are becoming more and more important.

In every corporate job I've had, I've found myself placed in the role of training new employees, not only because I seemed to have the patience required to teach others, but also because my method of teaching was to explain the *this-is-why* of what I was showing them, and not only the *do-it-because-that's-just-how-it-is*.

This is how I speak to my children as well. I

believe that for anything to "stick" and be understood at any level, the reasons and causes must be seen and known. Scientists agree, and often barely eat or sleep until they solve the riddle of why something they are observing is behaving as it is.

As more and more people are tiring of the old ways, they are beginning to question *everything*. They are beginning to want to know why they've been doing what they've been doing. The more they look back upon their lives and analyze the starting points of each conditioning, the more they discover it was *dictated* to them. They were told to do it. They kick themselves now and say, *"Why, oh, why did I just follow along with that back then?"*

And this is where the road forks.

From here, they have the choice to either blame others and shift the responsibility, or admit to and own their part in that history, accepting the responsibility of the fact they followed the influences pressed upon them. Even if the blind following was from a place of young naivety, it was still their responsibility — not as in a guilty "punishable blame" sort of way, but as in a "these are simply the facts of what happened." When one takes responsibility for and accepts their own reality instead of pointing the finger outside themselves, they take up their power and their birthright, and this is the starting point of changing the world.

Wait — the *world?*

Yes. The world.

You are the world. The entire world exists in *your* mind. What you think of the world, you create — both your personal perception of it, and the literal perception of it that others are able to "pick up on" and pass along.

The accusation that someone is wearing "rose-colored glasses" is based on the knowledge that whatever "mood" your thinking is in at any given moment is the flavor of perception you will see as you go about your day. If you hold a view that the world is dangerous and horrible, focusing on these things the majority of your time, you will naturally see anything that happens in this negative light. Something someone may do for you purely out of the kindness of their heart will be met with suspicion, and anything positive you hear will be automatically countered in your mind with its disastrous and worst-case potential opposite.

On the other side of that coin, to wear rose-colored glasses is to always look for the positive in all things. Encouraging and uplifting views are sought, and if there is nothing positive about a particular event or occurrence to be found, these "Pollyannas" then shift their thoughts to something directly related that they *can* view positively.

It is important to note here that each of these characters are extreme and opposite ends of the spectrum—each unbalanced alone in itself. A balanced and healthy Lightworker's goal is to rest in the middle ground somewhere between these two.

All the world is made of various forms of energy, including yourself. Everything from your physical body to the electricity in your brain is energy. The energy you choose to run through your being radiates from you like a sun, and hovers in the air like a cloud, influencing and coloring the environment around you. This reflects back to you as you observe the world around you. Then, when someone else comes along and walks through the energy cloud you've projected, they can easily absorb it and pick up on it. If something within them exists to match with the energy cloud, they could agree with it and take it on as their own, adding it to their own cloud projection, continuing the cycle.

An illustration for all this is in the wake of natural disasters. I was born and raised in Oklahoma, and am no stranger to tornadoes. The most recent tragedy my community went through together was the EF5 tornado whose most destructive peak tore through the city of Moore on May 20, 2013. In the aftermath of such power, many easily slipped into the angry, fearful thinking of "How could this have happened? Why us? This world is *too* dangerous! What sort of God would allow people — including *babies* — to be killed this way? We've *got* to get out of here."

When people have lost their homes, their loved ones, and even their own lives, what could possibly be seen as positive in this?

Nothing.

But what will dwelling on these accomplish? Beyond the healthy and necessary mourning process, what good will sitting in these facts of destruction do?

It will cultivate fear, despair, anger, and depression. And it will add those energies to your cloud, which will add it to your immediate environment, which will add it to your world.

You are the world.

What *can* be done with this situation then, if there is no positivity in it?

We are able to begin "spiraling out."

As Lightworkers, we do not wish to pollute our world with dark clouds of negativity. We've got no room for doom and gloom. Instead, we shift our vision outward. We search the edges of the matter, seeking the energy of the light — the positive — and feed our power to that, encouraging it to flourish into a flame. It is *always* there.

In the case of the tornado, considering the massive seventeen mile span of damage the two hundred and ten miles per hour winds inflicted, the thousands of people affected, and the billions of dollars in property destroyed, the fact that a mere twenty-three people actually lost their lives seems against *all* odds! Isn't the fact that only twenty-three people were lost as the deadliest recorded tornado in history to date ripped straight through a middle-of-the-day everyone-at-work-and-school heavily populated town *amazing?*

Hundreds of survival stories also came out of that day, and honoring these is another excellent way of changing the energy.

Shifting our view to the gratefulness of these incredible facts begins to allow us to release the heavy negativity and fear of the event, and to open to the positive, light energies present. The Lightworker coaxes this energy forward, fans its flame, and holds the vibration for others who are willing to also pick it up and pass it on.

This is how you begin to heal and change this world—by choosing to change *yourself.* The process of this can definitely burn, yet fragment by fragment, you begin to purify the energies of this place *through* your own self, and "where two or more are gathered" in this common cause, the greater and more powerful the healing grows.

This method of shifting your focus and choosing your view is by no means encouraging or justifying the "fingers-in-the-ear, *la-la-la* I can't hear you!" behavior. This is *not* an avoidance of reality — the negative *is* very present and real — but rather, it is an acknowledging and *accepting* of the reality as the fact that it is, yet choosing to work *with* it.

You will hear many arguments on these concepts. You may be accused of minimizing a catastrophe, or disrespecting the hurting and the dead. You could even be painted as cold and heartless for not continuing to wail in the rubble with them.

But the reality you will know in your Heart — and that the others will eventually see, as they themselves hopefully grow beyond the grief — is not that you have not acknowledged the tragedy, but that you *have* acknowledged it. You have accepted it as the fact that yes, this is what happened, this is where we are in this moment because of it, and therefore *this* is where we need to go in order to heal from this place. We flow ever forward.

There is a popular belief that says if you look at something or acknowledge it, it gives it power and increases its influence. This is simply not true, and is an act of fear and an avoidance of responsibility — a justification of running away, singing, "I did not just see that!"

The truth of the matter is not that we are afraid the power and strength of something "bad" will increase when we acknowledge it. The truth is we are afraid we will be required to *do* something about it. The encoding a Lightworker carries within their DNA is naturally drawn to search out and expose the "dark" areas of this place. But how can anything be exposed and changed if we are unwilling to even admit its existence?

We have all incarnated at a peak shifting point of this physical plane. The energies of this time are presenting everyone with circumstances and opportunities to face and disintegrate their fears at an ever-increasing rate. We are being given a clear choice: accept responsibility and take charge of our own life, or return to the beginning of the cycle, remaining in lower, disempowered states of being. This is what the over-hyped, fear-wrapped "2012 Shift" energies were about, and continue to be about. This shifting began long before 2012, and will continue as we progress into the twenty-first century.

Many are finding themselves unable to handle the "stepping up" of these energies, and are cracking, hiding, or straight out leaving. Because of this, those who *are* finding the strength to adjust and acclimate to this New Age are also discovering they are needed beyond simply taking care of themselves. This has the potential to activate their "human half," the self-preserving part of the ego that says "Whoa, now hold on here just a darn-tootin' minute! You want me to do *what?*"

To be asked to change the self in order to change the world burns the human ego.

To be asked to change the self and give even more to other people burns it even more — at least in the beginning.

As we adapt and consciously embody the "Light-headed" (another pun intended!) mentality, the self-preservation instincts of the ego begin to relax and see that it is not really being threatened, that it is not going to be obliterated by this work. Our eyes are further unclouded and able to see both ourselves and others from a deeper place of clarity.

When you are able to expose even the hidden and "undesirable" parts of yourself *to* yourself, as you *change* yourself, you will then have no difficulty or shame in exposing them to the world as you open wide to shine the Light of yourself.

It all begins with you.

ONE OF THE MOST misunderstood portrayals of the Lightworker is the image of the "woo-woo, sparkly, goody-goody" dancing among the flowers, calling out things like *"Blessings!"* and *"Namaste!"* as they wave their crystals and burn their incense. Just as television and media often project misleading stereotypes onto certain groups of people, it seems the stereotype of the "Pollyanna" extreme has been pinned to the Lightworker in people's minds. Being Light does *not* have to mean being "fluffy."

Lightworkers themselves don't help matters when they answer the world's crises and questions with responses like *"Just ask the archangels to come help you,"* and *"All you have to do is think it, and it will come true!"* These are certainly legitimate concepts that touch on points of truth, but when stated out of context, and to those who do not understand or believe these things, it only seems to confirm the view of the Lightworker as an unrealistic fool with their head in the clouds.

Acknowledging a disaster or difficulty, as mentioned in the previous chapter, is an important key that will help others understand your behavior as a Lightworker. Too often, they see and hear only the after-acknowledgement behavior and words. The acknowledging and recognizing must be repeated and continued throughout the process. It must be made clear that you are in no way belittling what happened by choosing to be positive and encouraging.

This is simply one example of many scenarios where I've seen Lightworkers misunderstood.

It is very important to develop a strong sense of discernment and awareness of both yourself and the audience in front of you each moment. If you are at a metaphysical expo or a spirit fair, surrounded by those of a like mind, you can freely "let yourself hang out," but if you are at a public mall, or perhaps your place of work, it may be more wise and mindful to choose your words and actions more carefully.

Is this being authentic?

Does this seem like an inauthentic hiding of yourself?

Aren't we taught to "let our Light shine" bright?

The purpose of this sort of discernment is not meant to deceive, but to *love*. Shining your Light does not mean beating others over the head with it—that would be the equivalent of the "cramming down your throat" methods some religious groups employ. No one responds well to bludgeoning.

Instead, you show love and mindfulness to those around you each moment by being the *type* of light they need in the present situation. If you're developing snapshots in a photography dark room, you need a red safe-light, not the sickly yellow-green of a fluorescent light. If you're manning a lighthouse on an island off the coast of Maine, you need a massive lamp and reflectors, not a tiny seven-watt night light bulb.

Meeting others on whatever level they are on in their life is not a lowering of yourself. All you have worked for will not be lost if you "stoop down" to meet another at a stage in their journey that you have already passed through in your own journey—in fact, doesn't it make even more sense that you will be able to help someone through a difficult time even more if you've already walked that way yourself? This is another difficulty Lightworkers often struggle with.

The dualistic labeling view of "higher than" and "lower than," and the thinking of "I am further, they are behind" is dangerous ground for a Lightworker, and to be avoided at all costs. Such separation invites judgment into the energy field, and opens the way for arrogant and elitist behavior to easily creep in. The best doctors see their patients not as "clients" or "cases," but as people — no different than they themselves are.

No level of any journey is any "better" or "worse" than any other. All stages are merely stepping stones along the way. Some will step on every stone, others will skip a couple, and still others will step backwards a bit, before moving forward once again. All are necessary, depending on the individuality of each person. Loving understanding is the aura of the Lightworker, radiating patience and openness to all, seeing no differences.

A scientist may visit an elementary school for a special presentation, but will she speak to the children using the professional terms and language she uses in the laboratory, or will she communicate the same knowledge in ways a third-grader will better understand? She will simplify her explanations, of course — but does this mean she's thrown all her years of training and experience out the window? On the contrary, it is *because* of her extensive experience she is able to translate the material to another level of understanding.

In the same way, the Lightworker is mindfully aware of where those around them are currently at in their processes and journeys, and translates whatever they understand to that level. It is not a "dumbing down," but simply an interpreting between languages.

The more you pay attention to and get to know those around you and their ways of thinking, the better you can interpret across the bridge of belief.

I was raised in a very strict Baptist household. I know and understand that way of life in a way that can only be fully comprehended by being completely immersed in it—living and breathing it. As I grew older and began asking questions to "find myself," and began searching to discover exactly what *I* personally believed in my heart—what resonated with *my* soul—the more I grew into *this* me, fully knowing *this* way of life. Because of this, translating between the Christian and the Metaphysical comes easily and naturally to me. When I'm having a conversation with my Christian friends and family, I can translate in my mind what they are saying in their language, apply and understand it in my own personal language, then communicate my perspectives and responses back to them rendered in words they are comfortable with.

This is another place that the understanding of the energy behind words becomes important. If you realize that it is the energy being communicated that is the "meat" of the matter, then you will easily be all right with replacing the word *Universe* or *Spirit* with the word *God*, for example — it is understood that both people are referring to *that great, all-encompassing energy*.

Again, the purpose and necessity of this is not to deceive, or even to "convert" anyone to your personal view — that is only *your* view — but simply to communicate, which is one of the first steps toward peace, love, and yes, Light.

Patience is the most important — and often most missing — key for a Lightworker working directly with others. They feel they have already been down that road and "done their time" with certain points, and they grow restless as they experience it again with others they're interacting with. The Lightworker's best view is once again gratefulness, returning to the "spiraling out," and choosing to find and focus on the positive of the situation.

Even when you have passed a certain period of growth yourself, if you can find the space to feel gifted by the opportunity to once again reflect on those experiences, you may find it very validating and empowering. You will realize just how far you *have* come, which will inspire you onward all the more, in the fullness of joy.

• 4 •
THE POWER

THE MORE YOU GROW "into yourself" as a Lightworker, the greater your awareness of the world and the energies around you will increase. Everyone has the ability to be a Lightworker, though it is a completely free will choice, even for those born feeling the "calling" yank at their Heart-strings.

Regardless of whether they arrived at the place of being a Lightworker naturally by "birth" or by a conscious, life-changing choice, each person will always have different levels of sensitivity to these energies than anyone else around them. Some will be more aware of the emotions and auras of individual people they cross paths with, and others will be more in tune with the energy and mass consciousness of society as a whole, the energies of the Earth herself — or all of the above. These diverse levels of ability are no different than the way some are able to run marathons tirelessly, while others are more adept at sitting motionless, programming computers all day. The runner may be horrible with computers and the programmer may lose a race to a snail, but both are valid humans. Both are still able to contribute to society in their own ways.

Does it *truly* matter if someone is more "psychic," while another is more "empathic?"

Does it *really* matter that your ear can't taste, and your toe can't smell?

Equality is another major goal the Lightworkers are here to demonstrate — and a huge reason why the awareness and discernment of energies is so important. When you can sense where another is mentally, psychologically, or emotionally as you interact with them, you will naturally be able to know much more clearly exactly how far their "boxes" can be stretched, and how deep their "buttons" can be pushed — or how "woo-woo" you can be around them.

Another reason discernment, or energy reading, is so important to cultivate is so you will be aware of exactly what others *do* need in the moment.

The absolutely outstanding 2013 DreamWorks Animation film *The Croods* illustrates this beautifully. The father of the family had been lost in a dangerous time, and the eldest daughter remained on the edge of the cliff, blowing her conch shell for him, waiting for him, watching for any sign of her father. The rest of the family had moved a bit ahead, then turned around. "It's not safe here," one said. "We have to keep moving." The old grandmother sadly nodded. "I'll go tell her." She went back to the eldest girl, and opened her mouth to deliver the news, then stopped. She felt something at that moment, "read" something in the daughter's energy. She sensed that, danger or no danger, this was not what the girl needed to hear at this time. So the grandmother said nothing at all, raised her own conch shell to her lips, and instead joined the girl in sounding her grief. A moment later, another shell sounded, then another and another, until the rest of the family one by one stepped up together, mourning as one. This is what the girl needed, in that moment, rather than being told to "cheer up and move on."

This empathic energy reading is not "reading other people's minds," or invading their privacy in any way. It is simply a bit more enhanced version of the ordinary ability every single human has. When you walk into a room, you can immediately sense the energy of it—is it awkward, comfortable, tense, relaxed? When you encounter a coworker, or another customer in the grocery store, you can *feel* what sort of mood they're in automatically—are they angry, depressed, joyful, exhausted? In both examples, you are sensing and "reading" the energies.

As a Lightworker, your ability to pick up on energies will typically heighten dramatically over time—not from any special super-powers you receive, but as a result of the work you do on *yourself*, first and foremost. Your starting point in everything is always *you*, and as you clear yourself out, purging anything discovered to be inauthentic, outdated, or harmful one by one, the clarity and space you create makes room to allow the energies of everything else into your awareness.

At times, feeling so much excess energy on top of your own energy and emotions can become quite overwhelming. The urge to run away or close down can get to be so strong that many stop trying to cope with it, or quit trying to find their balance. Some give up and sequester themselves away in a monastery to meditate all day, every day. Some find and hook into an intentional living community "off the grid," to attempt to avoid contact with the world. Others fly to some exotic country that has been placed on a pedestal as a spiritual paradise, such as India or Bhutan, to escape the "troubles" they have in their daily lives.

And what do all these eventually discover?

All the "noise," all the "interference," is in those places, just the same.

The source of your world is *you*, and wherever you go, there *you* are. You cannot run from your difficulties, and in claiming the title of Lightworker for yourself, you have accepted the responsibility to be authentic and committed, no matter what. You, above any other, must demonstrate the example of *facing* the difficulty, *doing* the work, *clearing* the way.

You do not have to travel to a faraway land in order to clear, balance, heal, or enlighten — whatever you feel you need most in this moment is with you right here, right now. In most cases, even *where* you need to be is right here, right now.

A Lightworker is an agent of change, an agent of healing, whether that healing requires a soothing and mending, or an exposing and ripping apart. A Lightworker is present to change systems, to encourage the evolution of a world, whether that world is seen or unseen. A Lightworker is born into, surrounded by, and led to wherever needs the power most, whether that need is met easily, or accomplished with blood, sweat, and tears. A Lightworker will feel the call to do whatever is needed in whatever system they find themselves in — from *within* that system. What will running away accomplish, except possible suffering on all sides?

The awareness that they are public examples of conscious living can easily drive a Lightworker to strive for perfection. They begin to feel they cannot afford to ever make a mistake, and sometimes slowly begin to adopt a sort of rigid and paranoid routine. If this obsessive behavior is not confronted and attended to for a long period of time, it can begin to block the energetic flow of insight and intuition the Lightworker must be able to feel in order to remain in tune with what is going on around them, and know where they might be able to make a difference. They try to be a "superhero," pushing themselves above and beyond their limits — *ignoring* their limits — attempting to achieve this unrealistic state, and present themselves as the model of perfection.

This is inauthentic, and will eventually crumble through the same way a relationship will when one or both partners put on an act, building themselves up to be better and larger than life in the early stages of the relationship. It is impossible for the ruse to last forever, and will ultimately evaporate, revealing the truth behind the facade, dissolving the relationship with it.

Imagine you discover a baby bird has fallen from its nest and its mother has abandoned it. Seeing it is unable to fly yet, or find food for itself, you take the baby home. You feed it many times throughout the day. It survives, and grows bigger and stronger, until it is ready to learn to be a bird. You pick it up and place it next to your goldfish. Days go by, and the baby bird still has not learned to be a bird, and in fact now lowers its head and wiggles its tail feathers — like a fish!

You realize then, as you laugh at the sight of a bird mimicking swimming, that a goldfish could never have demonstrated how to fly. It only knows about swimming.

This is essentially what a superhero trying to show the best way to be a human is like. It is completely unrealistic. Inspiration, higher aspirations, and role models *are* very important to have in order to keep growing, but to measure up to something as mis-matching and unattainable as a superhero — like a fish teaching a bird to fly — is to invite and inspire thoughts of "failure," when failure is a complete illusion, based on perception alone.

How then can a human be an example to other humans?

By being *human*.

By being *fearlessly* human.

When you begin at the starting point of yourself, examining and eliminating ideas, behaviors, and beliefs that no longer serve your highest good, your human ego has the tendency to panic and try to sweep these "mistakes" under the rug, afraid you will be judged or looked down upon. It feels what "good" things you *have* done will be discredited or belittled if such "scandals" are exposed. It encourages the thoughts of *"I must be spotless and perfect in every* way."

But what better way to relate to those you are trying to reach than sitting in their midst, openly showing that *you are no different?* Isn't this what every great spiritual teacher of history and myth-tory has displayed?

And if you who are "flawed" and have done some not-so-Light things in the past can attain a clarity and balance within yourself, and reach the level of Lightworker through hard work and determination, then maybe there *is* a chance for them as well.

Expose yourself.

Shine your Light.

Let them see that you, too, have difficult days, bad moods, confusing times.

This is *Grace.*

The only way anyone can change is by their own free will, when they are ready, when *they* choose. The example and the inspiration the Lightworker provides may be the lighting of the fuse, but it is completely up to each individual to allow that spark to reach the dynamite and shatter their lives and their boxes or not—no one else can do it for them.

Just as psychologists and counselors watch their clients very closely to see whether they are absorbing, shifting, and applying what has been discussed and analyzed in their sessions, so must the Lightworker, when working to assist another.

If they see that they are the only one doing all the work, and the one they are trying to help or heal is just "riding along," making no effort of their own, the interaction must be cut off.

Many argue that this brand of "tough love" is cruel, or "giving up" and abandoning the one in need. But is it really? Which is the greater benefit to all involved — empowering someone to make their own choice of whether to do the work or not, thereby placing their responsibility into their own hands, or you continuing to carry them on your back, thereby draining and exhausting yourself and disempowering them? One way releases you and strengthens — or at least correctly places accountability on — the other, and the alternative disempowers and traps yourself while enabling the other to continue avoiding responsibility.

A doctor does not prescribe the required medicine, then go to the pharmacy with you, make sure you buy the medicine, go home with you, and stand over you to see that you take the proper dosage at the proper times until the bottle is empty and you are cured. Imagine how tired the doctor would be if they did everything for you. Think of all the other patients that would suffer from finding the doctor away from his office and unable to treat them! And wouldn't the doctor's family feel neglected as well?

Instead, the doctor merely prescribes the

medicine, and sends you on your way. From that point, the responsibility is entirely in your hands.

In reality, no one can truly do anything for anyone else. The only one anyone can do anything for is themselves.

To love someone does not mean to do all things for them, or even to *allow* all things with them. In fact, true love will *not* allow another to remain dependent and disempowered. The power of Love — and a Lightworker — is often wrapped in the life-nurturing act and words of *"Now you're on your own."*

Lights are placed in darkness.

Even if a room is well lit, there may still be shadows or darker corners that require an additional lamp or torch, depending what period of history you live in.

Yet even if there are a thousand lights in a room, there will still eventually be darkness. Electric lights can shine all through the night — *if* they have power. Electricity is never guaranteed forever. You could have a hundred back-up generators in line, ready to keep the power on if the world ends, but eventually even those will be used up, and darkness will be seen again.

A Lightworker is placed in darkness. A Lightworker is *needed* in darkness.

A Lightworker does not run from the darkness, hiding and avoiding the "yucky" feel of it. Lightworkers operate from a higher frequency of energy vibration, so it is only to be expected that the contrasting lower, "darker" energy vibration feels just that much more repelling to them.

Most of the time, a balanced Lightworker is "shielded" or unaffected by the darkness around them. They are able to be "in the world, but not *of* the world," moving through their environment, transmuting what lower vibrations are washed over them. But the wise Lightworker also knows and understands that journeys are not one straight upward line to the top of Ascension Mountain—it is much more like a roller coaster climbing, then dropping down its track, before climbing to the next peak. There will always be dips. There will always be dark times.

My close friend, Jennifer, is an accomplished mountain climber. She has participated in expedition after expedition, braving even the toughest ice and snow. She's told me story after story of these adventures, and one of the things that surprised me at first—a misconception I found I had about mountain climbing—was that they cannot simply climb straight up and *ta-dah!* reach summit. They must first make it to a certain point, a particular elevation, and then make camp. From there, the rest of the journey is done in steps, or shifts—some in the party will scout ahead, perhaps carrying a bit of the supplies, and set up a smaller camp before going back down to the first camp. Then the first camp will be packed up, and everyone will move on ahead to that second camp, which becomes "first camp" as the process repeats over and over, until the summit is reached. Up, then down, then up again; forward, then backward, then forward again.

When this is the reality of any sort of progress or journey, why does "two steps forward, one step back" have such a negative reputation?

Whether you are in the midst of an external darkness, or you are dealing with your own personal difficulties, there will always be dark times. And if this is known and seen from experience to be true — even expected — then the darkness will hold no power over you. It will then simply become an *"Oh! Would you look at that — it's a rough day today,"* rather than a crippling, crumbling devastation to you.

There is an old saying under Oklahoma's fickle atmosphere: "If you don't like the weather, just wait a minute." Several times in my life here I've been outdoors, stomping through snow drifts in simply a t-shirt, as it was twenty degrees and snowing all one day, then sunny and sixty-five degrees the next.

It is incredibly easy for the human mind to feel as if whatever is going on in the moment is permanent and how things are going to be forevermore, although this can be seen to be clearly untrue. The mind has the habit of focusing down to one narrow sliver of time, and treating it as if it is the new world. Yet, as you look back over your life, you will see that no "bad" time has ever lasted, the same way no "good" time has ever lasted. All things are in constant motion, and change is the *only* constant, the only dependable and permanent thing in this world.

When you are going through a dark time in your life, it may seem as if all is lost, all is doomed. Emotions may clamp a death grip on you, making it difficult for you to attain the higher-view clarity and insight you might be able to reach quite easily under normal circumstances. The mind gathers up its collected views and fears, and feeds them into the emotion pit. The emotions then feed the fears and doubts back to the mind, which in turn feeds them right back into the emotions in a spiraling cycle of gloom.

Emotions arise from the mind. Mind *makes* the emotions. "What goes in is what comes out" is very true. In the same way you steer your outward thoughts to focus on what you choose — the positive — you can also choose what thoughts you allow inward. Worry, fear, doubt, resentment, and anger can be your first response when you're thrown for an unexpected loop, or your habitual responses can be filled with positive, confident viewpoints that allow you to remain clear-minded when "disaster" strikes. The importance of positive content and clear view cannot be stressed enough. A mature, wise, and logical mind will be able to view the situation helpfully to begin with, while a mind that has been focused on all that is "wrong" with the world, jumping to every fear-based, worst-case scenario, will more easily and quickly shut down when things do not go as expected.

Negativity, violence, and hatred will always be around. There is no way to completely avoid it as it swirls around you—you have no control of things and others outside yourself—but yourself is what you *can* control. If your senses are assaulted with something frightening or threatening, it is your choice whether it is allowed to sink into your "operating system," or if it is deflected as *"Yes, this has happened, this is acknowledged, but I do not agree with it and I refuse to allow it to compose my reality."*

Anything you adopt, you amplify and pass on in your own energy field, adding it to the collective reality of the planet. When you refuse to contribute to the negativity, you are taking responsibility for the part you *can* play, making a difference in this world, whether it is immediately noticeable or not. Many people often expect or want immediate results in everything, and this is no exception.

The dark times are necessary, although there are those who argue that it is not. Some imagine and strive for a perfect Utopia where conflict is nonexistent, and change is nowhere to be found. But in reality, how balanced is that? That concept is only one extreme end of the spectrum.

The Wachowski Brothers understood this truth, and placed it in their smash hit 1999 Warner Bros. Film, *The Matrix*. When the agent had captured Morpheus, he revealed that that version of the Matrix program was not the first version—the initial programs had been a perfect society for the minds of the humans the machines had enslaved. But the human minds would not accept the picture-perfect perfection, and kept trying to "wake up out of it." The machines learned from this, and re-wrote the program to contain chaos, stress, and balance— "imperfection." The human minds were then able to accept the holographic programming.

How will the light be known without the dark? Without the differences between night and day, there would be no words for "night" and "day"—it would be all light all the time, or all dark all the time, with no reason to label any distinctions otherwise. Time would only be dates on a calendar. Day and night cannot exist without each other, just as the positive cannot be known without the negative.

"Then what is the point of working so hard to bring more Light to this plane?" you ask. "Isn't *that* a negative viewpoint to say there will always be darkness?"

Well, is it horrible that night comes every… night? On the contrary, the period of night is necessary for the cycles of our own bodies. The calmness and rest are important for the health of our physical body.

Even if this is only because we have evolved and adjusted to — gotten used to — having a dark period, this still serves as example of how we are able to adapt to the environment we find ourselves in. Do we try to fight the night? Are we searching for ways to conquer and eliminate the rotation of the earth, so we don't have to look at the darkness? Even if that were possible, someone on the other half of the planet would still be in the dark.

The contrasts of "dark" and "light" return us back to the topic of perception. Each of these are simply levels of vibration — one a faster rate of vibration, the other, a slower rate.

So what is the point of working toward a higher, faster vibration of living then, if there will always be a lower, slower vibration? Everything is connected, and everything is relative. When one side raises, the other side raises. The "flipside" will always be the flipside, whether the coin is laying on the floor, or pinned to the ceiling. For example, if the "Light" side is currently at level seven, and the "Dark" side is at level two, there is a five-level distance between them. If the Light manages to ascend five levels to a twelve, the Dark will naturally also be raised five levels, to a seven—the very space the Light used to be! Yet because the Light is now at level twelve, level seven seems "low" and "dark."

In the same way, this current Light you live in was once at the level of the current Dark, and you know the Light from the Dark by their contrast.

This is necessary.

There will always be periods of darkness—power will black out, firewood will burn down, and suns will set. What is classically referred to as the "Dark Night of the Soul"—the human ego's difficulty in the shedding and shaking loose of all that no longer serves it—is also a necessary part of growth. It can seem very much like a "crash" or a "hitting of rock bottom." The burn the mind feels in releasing returns as the old melts away. This period can last for days, weeks, months, or even years, depending on each individual, and each situation. But as the night eventually passes into dawn, the new level on the other side is discovered, and the panic of the process disappears. You find it was indeed more than worth it all.

• 6 •
THE LIGHT

WHILE LIGHT SCATTERS THE darkness, it also has the ability to cast shadows. A shadow is simply the blocking of light from falling completely on an object—stand between the candle and the wall, and your body will absorb that part of the light shining out, creating a dark silhouette of you on the wall.

Shadows are one of the greatest fears many, many people have, whether physical, bump-in-the-night shadows, or the psychological and spiritual shadows within their own personality.

If our Light is considered to be our highest, truest self, then it follows that our Shadow is that which stands in the way of the fullness of our Light shining on the Wall of the World.

"Facing your Shadows," or doing your "Shadow Work" are currently popular catch-phrases in spiritual circles today. Unfortunately, the implications when this is discussed or mentioned are most often in the energy of pride and attention-getting. *"Hey look what I'm doing – I'm dealing with my shadow side!" "Oh, moan! I'm having such a miserable time trying to face my shadow self..." "You need to sit down and work with your shadow, man – I did, now look at me!"*

This is another area that breaks my Heart.

Just as the energy of a thing remains the same no matter what it's called, the energy of your intentions is unable to be altered. On the surface, things may appear to be one way, but if you are able to look deep enough, the energy underneath cannot lie.

And the energy of these particular examples of prideful shadow-talk is no different than if you donated ten million dollars to a charity, and then called the press to have it announced in various publications. The donation would help others, sure – but how does that broadcast of your good deeds make *you* look? It essentially negates and cancels out any pureness that may have been present in what you did.

This is the same for anything you do, and should be a part of your daily authenticity self-examination. There are certain times that sharing the "story" of your struggle and journey is appropriate and will even encourage others still in the middle of similar journeys, but for the most part, these are your own private and internal battles, meant only for you. The intention and energy in sharing such things must be honest and pure, and not being used for attention or pity.

Facing your shadows is figuratively standing in front of a mirror, looking at yourself completely naked — wide open, and brutally honest with yourself. It is magnifying your "facts," and examining them with an open Heart to maturely determine what should then be done next — a determination of your *own* choosing, entirely up to you.

I use the word "facts" here rather than "flaws" or "imperfections" because these terms are dualistic and imply a negative "badness" or "wrongness" in you. "Good" and "bad" are concepts that have been ingrained in our minds, but are ultimately illusions based on ideas that are relative, and cannot always be depended on. No blanket definition can ever cover every situation and every case in anything. Even so, finding another word without so many connotations attached will help you step around the hang-ups of a particular word, such as replacing the word "flaws" with the word "facts."

Another word with heavy blocking energy around it is the word "money." Centuries of different energies regarding money have built up around this word, and frequently jam people up, creating personal issues for them in obtaining and managing it. Fear, greed, and lack have encased it in layers of difficult energy that some have a hard time cracking through. But if they can shift the word in their thinking about it from "money" to "cash" or "moolah," they may then be able to shift their internal and often subconscious reaction to it, and side-step the blockage.

So to face your shadows, you sit with yourself, and examine your facts, just as they are, raw and exposed. You muster your courage, grit your teeth, and — as painful as it can feel at times — fearlessly look at yourself as you are, without judgment, deception, or flattery.

And this is meditation.

This is the original purpose of meditation — to silence all the voices in and around you, to still every mask and personality you wear, and turn within to examine yourself in your naked state. Regrettably, many people seek the calm, quiet edge of meditation, and stop there, like a peace junkie, getting their "fix."

Why would you examine your facts so closely? Because you can. Because you have the power to. Because you have the responsibility of your own self, because you have the power to pick and choose your own self, and because you *can* pick and choose who you are.

Do you like all you see?

Do you see a — *gasp!* — shadow?

Move even closer to the places you don't like and choose to make different within you, then search for ways you may begin to change those into something more to your liking. Shift a word or thought pattern. Put your foot down and stop something. Or pick your foot *up*, if you need to *start* something. It's all trial-and-error. Hypothesize, experiment, observe, adjust, experiment again — and there is no wrong way or right way. There is only *your* way.

This is shadow work.

Many of our shadows come with us pre-installed. Some are inherited, passed down our genetic line. Others are learned, whether from observing and adopting, or experiencing, adapting, and reacting. However they develop and grow within us, every single person carries these built-in tools of growth, meant to push us further in our journeys by shining light on what we *do* want, in the roundabout way of displaying to us what we *do not* want.

Light makes shadows.

The Light exposes shadows.

The Lightworker is committed to clearing their shadows, and living as authentically as possible. This alone raises their vibration, which in turn raises the vibrations around them, which in turn raises the vibration of the planet. They cannot do anyone else's work for them — especially another person's shadow work.

Self-honesty is a very important key when doing self-work. When a shadow is discovered, the habitual reaction may always be to point the blame outside yourself, saying, *"Surely I could not have created or invited this!"*

But only what energy vibrations match each other can exist in the same space. For something to attract to something else, there has to be some part in each that resonates and syncs up. When something is going on in your life, pause and honestly ask yourself *"Is there anything inside myself that could have matched and allowed this?"*

This is what is meant when the world and all around you is referred to as a "mirror" for yourself. Every person you meet, every event you experience, every single thing that enters your awareness holds the possibility of being a mirror held in front of you, reflecting pieces of yourself back to you that you may be too close to see otherwise.

The mirror is in no way meant to accuse, shame, or punish—that will accomplish nothing but a tearing down. Instead, its intention and purpose is to inspire growth at the strength of your own hand. What is shown to you are simply the facts, here and now. Your daily starting point.

You choose where to go from there.

— PART II —

THE **WORKER** PART

• 7 •
THE SHOCK

Even IN THE MOVIES, the hero — the "good guy" — does, and is willing to do, whatever is necessary for the safety of others. A major misconception about Lightworkers is that they are always timid, nonviolent, and therefore defenseless people who will "turn the other cheek," no matter the cost. This is most likely an extension of the "fluffy" stereotype.

But Lightworkers are the ones actually doing the hardest work, whether behind the scenes, or on the front lines — far from shallow fluffiness.

The concept of "nonviolence" is often confused and assumed to mean "never-violence." The image of Mahatma Gandhi and the way he chose to use silent civil disobedience and peaceful non-cooperation to take a stand against corruption immediately comes to people's minds at the mention of this word.

While Gandhi's determination *was* from an unshakeable belief that all violence is evil, no matter what, can this truly apply in every situation as a black-and-white blanket code of ethics? Is it really possible to be able to promise you will never do any harm to any creature on any level, no matter what?

Can you ensure your feet are missing every ant and flea as you stroll through your yard — even if you are doing a walking meditation?

Are you positive the spider whose source of catching dinner was just destroyed will survive as a result of your accidentally passing through her web?

What if an intruder breaks into your house while your family is home? Will you stand by and allow your daughter to be taken, or worse?

How do you guarantee that nothing you say or do will ever spark a reaction in someone else's own little world, as they operate in whatever conditioning their life has colored their perception with?

There is no way to make sure you will never cause some level of harm to anyone or anything — but you *can* make sure your intentions are truly well-meaning, and that your greatest aim is to not cause harm, *if it can be avoided in any way.*

Nonviolent means *wishing* and *intending* no harm in any way, and avoiding it wherever possible. But sometimes, to stubbornly stand by and do nothing just because the action that may stop some greater harm might be considered to be violent or harmful on any level is another imbalanced, extreme end of the spectrum. This is not to say that violence solves the problem of violence, but that there may be times when defense of yourself or others is required. Sometimes you may just have to do what you have to do, or greater and broader suffering can occur. Gandhi's form of nonviolence happened to work beautifully in that particular situation, but would that honestly work in, say, today's Middle Eastern regions? If they all decided to just sit down and refuse to participate, would the war and hatred just go away? They would all be slaughtered.

No two situations are ever alike. There are hundreds of angles, perspectives, and contributions that factor into each scenario — how can any one absolute blanket answer fit each and every case? This applies to everything everywhere. There are no absolute answers or rules — only the most beneficial options and concepts to strive for.

The hero knows this, and is prepared to do whatever is in his power to do his job. Yet at the same time, he is not *attached* to it. He is wise enough to recognize when something will be a waste of time or energy, or to see when something will be impossible without harming himself — and how will he then be able to help anyone or anything else ever again if he is harmed? The hero knows himself and his own limits better than anything else. It is his — and the Lightworker's — responsibility to keep himself healthy and balanced first and foremost, or he will not be able to help anyone else.

This is not selfishness, but wisdom.

In fact, it could even be taken so far as to say that standing by and doing nothing simply to maintain a misconceived form of nonviolence is much more selfish than taking care of *yourself* first.

"Turning the other cheek" is not a phrase meaning to passively allow all things to continue no matter what, or even to embody the military training mentality of *"Thank you, Sir! May I have another please, Sir!"*

Turning the other cheek refers to not holding anger and resentment toward one who has wronged you, to not retaliating in revenge, and to extending forgiveness and understanding where no forgiveness and understanding is deserved. This is called "patient forbearance," but in no way means the continued allowance of a wrong — it does not simply "look the other way." The master guru in stories and movies illustrates this in the way they calmly show no reaction, no matter what is going on, until the exact moment is right to do or say something, usually stopping the other dead in their tracks, hit over the head with realization and insight.

In the many types of people and groups I've been around over the course of my journey so far, I've met many "darker" people who view "lighter" people as weak and pathetic because of the misconception that those of the Light will not defend themselves, much less fight back. They feel safe and secure in bullying Lightworkers for fun, trying to terrorize them just for the shock reaction, often depending on harsh, flustering tactics to try to get the other to lower their shielding in panic at the assault.

The misunderstanding of nonviolence and patient forbearance by *both* sides creates needless harm *on* both sides.

When a Lightworker *does* defend herself, and is able to protect herself and *maintain* her protection through an assault—or even prove stronger, able to stop the attacker in some way—the dark is shocked, and then has something to sit back and think about, perhaps even a reassessing of their own motives and drives.

The shamans of ancient times knew this. While they were healers of the village, they were also the protectors. In the same way they intuitively connected with the spirits of the land and animals for assistance in their healing and helping of the village, they would also receive messages from the spirit world and natural world warning of oncoming raids or attacks from other villages or wild animals, thus being able to prepare the village in advance, if not do something spiritually and energetically to put a stop to the imminent event before it ever arrived.

When necessary, they healed the people, saving lives. When necessary, they protected the people, taking lives. Yet they were revered as what would be called Lightworkers today.

Did they feel they needed to project an image of "light and fluffy" in order to fulfill their role? They knew their actions and results spoke louder than any words or portrayed images.

Just as love does not mean allowing all things no matter what, just for the sake of love, peace does not mean allowing all things no matter what, just for the sake of peace. Peace is not always nonviolent. Sometimes a piece of violence—meaning anything that could be considered "harm"—is required in order to reach a place of peace, but this does not justify performing immediate actions and reactions, done in anger or vengeance. Like the master guru, careful observing, analyzing, and applying insightful wisdom is required in each unique situation, before any action is to be taken. The "nonviolent" way is always sought, above all.

Two major keys in Lightworking are a detached, non-judgmental understanding, and a flowing flexibility. The Lightworker is a light, a flame. A flame is fire, which ultimately burns and consumes, and—if a fire is strong enough—even the wind cannot blow its flames out.

How does a fire resist the wind shoving it around? By standing against the forces of the air, as stiff and firm as a brick wall? Or does it survive, cope with, and even *work with* the wind by *moving* with it—dancing and twisting in the forces railing against it?

It keeps its grip on the wood by *going with the flow*—and it not only adapts to, but *needs* the air, absorbing its oxygen to survive and grow even stronger.

This is the way your flame as a Lightworker never goes out. Resistance will cause friction and suffering, but if you can go with the flow of what you cannot control around you, you will often find ways to adapt and make use of what is happening for the better. You may even stumble across a way to bring justice to an unjust situation from the inside, in a way you would never have been able to see or do while standing on the outside.

• 8 •
THE WORK

MOST OF THE "WORKER" part of "Lightworker" is just that—working light. Shining light, brightening areas, and shifting the energy of a place are things a Lightworker does naturally, simply by their very presence.

You may not even realize how many hundreds of times your simple smile at a stranger has made a complete difference in their life. You may never know if you've saved a life by holding the door open for someone you don't even know to enter ahead of you. You cannot disprove that the mere act of you walking into a room enlightened the energy enough that somebody on the brink of despair was relieved of their own oppressive energies long enough to find the exact insight they needed to shift their own world.

These few examples illustrate the natural and innocent ways you embody light on this planet.

You *are* a Light, and the most powerful and effective way you can *be* this Light is in innocent purity from the Heart, and not from the head — the purity that radiates smoothly, without thinking. Light ripples like waves on a pond. Everything touches everything, and everything affects everything.

But sadly, so often people wait until they *are* touched by something before they will give it any attention. If it doesn't involve them, if it doesn't affect them, if it's not in their immediate environment, they don't care. Until something happens directly to them or someone they know, it is not a "real" concern. When it *does* happen to their personal world, *then* they grow enraged at the injustice, and fight to change the system, or become determined to raise money to help find a cure — whatever action each case demands.

Why is there no care or advocacy until we are directly affected by something? Why do we wait until our own husband has cancer, until our own sister is raped, until our own child is attacked?

Don't we see?

Can't we hear?

Where is our compassion simply for the pure sake of compassion?

I've noticed the ideology of compassion in the minds of many people is misguided. The meaning of compassion in their eyes seems to border much more on the side of pity.

Compassion embodies the energy of *relating* within it—the honest kindness that comes from identifying with someone else, whether from your own personal experience in a similar situation, from the ability to fully imagine yourself in their shoes, or even because of the simple fact they are a living being, just as you are.

Pity suggests an air of superiority, and of "feeling sorry for" the other. Pity comes more from a space of believing you are better than the other, looking down on them, and considering them to be beneath you. This can be a subconscious thought, and stem from confusing *"I am better off than they are"* with *"I am better than they are."*

Acts done in this mentality are not from a pure, light, compassionate Heart, but from the perspective of *"Oh, you poor, helpless thing—let I who am so much better than you are help you out!"* This is the same level the human ego operates from—the same level that also loves to broadcast its good deeds for attention.

Pity encourages separation.

Compassion promotes equality.

The Lightworker is present for, and committed to enlightening this time, in whatever way they can. They allow their bright, free-flowing nature to lead them where they are needed most, doing what is needed most. True compassion is their motivating force, yet even in this, they must keep a watchful eye on themselves as well as all that is happening around them—the big picture. A Lightworker can feel a compassionate tug in nearly every direction at any given time, but if they follow a compassionate action at the cost of abandoning other, greater factors, including themselves and their *own* health and rest, then is the act truly worth it?

Mindfulness and discernment are the ticket.

If you choose to pass by a situation you could possibly help, *without* helping it, there will be no punishment or retribution coming to you. There is no guilt, blame, or shame to feel—those emotions will only drag and tear you down. This is not what "karma" is.

The Universe is even vaster than we can imagine in our wildest dreams, and in that vastness are infinite options and probabilities. Do you really believe that *you* were that situation's last and only hope?

There is choice in all things—free will. You are never demanded or commanded to do anything. You are merely presented with options you can either choose or not choose—it is *your* free will life to live.

Many understand the concept of karma as payback, punishment, or "The Revenge of the Universe," but none of these are quite the true meaning of karma.

While it's true that karma is a return of sorts, it is merely a "cause and effect" — one thing naturally resulting in another thing. If you choose to kick a soccer ball barefoot, you can certainly make that happen, but you might stub and hurt your toe in the process. Is that your punishment for kicking the ball, or is it simply the result of kicking the ball?

Another example of karma could be the way someone may spontaneously take a different route to work one morning, for no reason at all. Later, they hear there was a horrible accident at the exact point of the highway, at the exact time they would have been there if they had taken their usual route. They cannot explain why they took an alternate course that day, especially if they normally take the same route every single day.

This is often called "good karma."

How can good karma potentially prevent a disaster or an unwanted circumstance? Some believe that doing good deeds from a loving, compassionate, and selfless Heart will essentially "rack up" good karma, and eventually "burn off" any bad karma that may have accumulated in this life, as well as previous lives. This is a simple illustration of the energy of karma.

Just as whatever energy you choose to radiate through yourself forms an aura or cloud around you, in turn coloring and affecting the world around you, that energy also draws more of the same energy to you and your surroundings.

Like attracts like.

If you are worried and afraid a majority of your time, always watching and waiting for the next tragedy to strike, then that is the energy you will broadcast, and that is the energy that will answer—you will call your fears to you. The other way around, if your view is one that searches for and focuses on the positive and beautiful things that are always present even in the "dark" times, then you will seem to be able to soar right through difficult situations unharmed—not because the "bad" things haven't happened to you, but because you refuse to allow them to pull you down into the muddy pits of despair, depression, and negativity.

This energetic interaction between you and your environment is commonly called *The Law of Attraction*. What goes in comes out, and what goes out comes back—the Golden Rule. This applies to action, word, and thought forms.

In this way of understanding how our energy cooperates with the energy of the Universe at large, it may be easy for some with more negative, self-demeaning inclinations to take the Law of Attraction to the extreme, saying, *"So if everything around me is a result of the energy I put out, then all that is bad that happens to me is my own fault, and therefore I am to blame and must be* punished."

But this is another extreme that Lightworkers must watch for in others, and gently encourage them back to the middle, balanced ground. The knowledge and understanding that you create your own reality is not meant to point the finger of blame and tear you down, but meant to empower you to consciously choose your energy, attitude, and actions.

So in the example of the highway accident and their spontaneous, life-saving change of route, perhaps that person does their best to live and act from a compassionate Heart, always open to discovering ways of helping and caring for others.

Since that is the energy they put out—the cloud they form—then that is the energy they are tuned in to. It provides feedback to them in many ways, even if subconsciously. The person on the highway may have felt the impressed message of *"Don't go that way today"*—their good karma's "payback."

Of course, things are not always so plainly "cut-and-dry" as that example.

There is absolutely no way it can be said that all "good" things that happen to someone are because they did "good" things, and that all "bad" things that happen to them are because they did "bad" things. There are no absolute blanket answers for anything—there are simply too many contributing factors at play in all things. You can never know or track down every angle to determine every cause, and you could spend years debating different viewpoints, concepts, and beliefs.

This is not to say to not even *try* to examine and contemplate a situation to glean wisdom from it for future use, but if too much time and energy is given to a situation with too many factors—many of them unknown or unseen—it then becomes a waste of that precious present-moment time and energy.

Instead, your focal point should be the same as your starting point—yourself. Take care of yourself, and make sure you are as authentic as you can be, so the energy attracted back to you from your karmic energy cloud can be as beneficial as possible, and your work can be as effective as possible.

LIGHTWORKERS IN THIS DAY and age seem to be faced with more sadness, turmoil, and corruption than ever before. The news programs report mostly negative accounts of danger and destruction, with the exception of the latest celebrity gossip.

All these do nothing but instill and promote fear. Fear does nothing but instill and promote separation. Separation does nothing but instill and promote fear — a never-ending cycle.

Where have all the positive, encouraging, human-interest stories gone?

Why has everything become about the latest threat to your life, health, or income?

The greatest answer to this is *control.*

The possibility of a fear coming true is a quick and easy motivation to get something done. Afraid the storm rolling in will produce hail, and your car will get dented and smashed? You drop everything you're doing, and pull your vehicle into the garage in a hurry. Afraid your house will be broken into and you will be robbed of all your valuables? You have multiple locks and an alarm system installed as soon as possible. Afraid your heart will be broken again? You shy away from all future relationships.

The greatest built-in fear each person carries within them is the fear of losing their own control, or *sense* of control. When that power is threatened, the panic that floods their system can cause abnormal and sometimes irrational behavior. Those who seek control over others try to use this to their advantage through various methods of emotional or physical manipulation.

Bullies especially use these tactics repeatedly to manipulate their victim into doing what they want—figure out what someone's greatest fears are, and you have the power to control them.

In the same way, the media seems to keep its focus on the most awful, horrible, disturbing, and upsetting stories possible nearly full-time now. This keeps the people in a perpetual state of fear, and therefore more easily ready to do whatever those in control then declare is *The Thing To Do* in order to remain safe—to jump when they say jump.

The ultimate goal in this strategy is to keep the hope of the people downtrodden and squashed.

Hope is the greatest and most empowering thing—the spark to a fire that cannot be put out once it ignites, and this is the fire that rages within Hearts, granting the strength and bravery to squarely face any force, to stand up to any form of adversity or oppression. Hope is one of the controller's greatest enemies.

A very well-done series that demonstrates this is *The Hunger Games* trilogy by Suzanne Collins. The heroine of these dystopian, future-of-America stories, Katniss Everdeen, inadvertently inspires uprisings against the evil Capitol, simply by being her own independent, strong, compassionate self. She never set out to spark a rebellion, yet the mere example of her kindness to others and her unshakable dedication to do what was right gave the masses who watched her on screen a hope and a strength that the Capitol then fought to snuff out once again. Katniss shows us how it *is* possible for one person to begin a major change.

You may not be able to *make* the change in the world, but you can most definitely *start* the change. You may never see the outcome and end of it yourself, but you can see present-time clues that the change is in motion.

Attachment to the outcome is another method of trying to control your environment. You cannot always control everything, and in fact can rarely ever truly control anything. The reality is you merely *begin* everything, then release it to fly on its own, wherever the winds of the various influencing factors may blow it. Once you fold a paper airplane and launch it, you no longer have control of how it flies — you've surrendered it to the angles of its wing folding, and to the air currents of the room around you.

So the powers that be, backed by the media pumped into your home and your car, fight to keep your eyes averted from anything that may potentially empower you, so that they may dictate what is and isn't to be.

Is the answer then to be in fear of those in control? To merely give up and give in, submitting in hopelessness and despair, not trying at all? Conspiracy theorists may say so, as they devote every free moment to searching for corrupt and ulterior motives around every corner and behind every official person. Another branch on the extremity scale, conspiracy theorists can talk for hours on end about how useless it is to try anything except what is controlled by the authorities.

While there may be bits and pieces of truth in their stories and "reports," the fear mentality they induce is no better than the media feed — essentially two ends of the same stick.

It is all right to take action when it is called for. It is all right to protect yourself and your loved ones. It is all right to prepare for the future — the key is to do these things and whatever is necessary in the moment from a place of empowerment, wisdom, and discernment, not from a place of fear and desperation.

You are "enlightened" and above it all when you are able to live and move among all the extremes and fears and horrors and injustices, yet react to them from a place of fearlessness. It *is* possible to acknowledge, talk about, and even face all these things, *and* operate from a still, calm place of non-affectedness.

It is very important to keep up to date with current events and all that is going on in the world around you, but it is very important to do so from a higher viewpoint — with eyes focused on the bigger picture. As the mystic storyteller Kahlil Gibran so eloquently stated in his masterpiece *The Prophet*: "You shall be free indeed not when your days are without a care, nor your nights without a want or a grief, but rather when these things girdle your life, and yet you rise above them, naked and unbound."

Enlightenment is so often mistakenly expected to mean that there will be no troubles or hardships or heartaches. It is misunderstood that once you attain enlightenment, all things will fall into place almost magically, and nothing will ever be "bad" again.

But it is not the outside world that changes when you reach enlightenment—it is *you* that changes. *Your* perceptions shift, *your* world view changes, *your* ego stops driving the bus.

The things all around you stay the same. Your reaction to them is what "enlightens."

Instead of reacting to fears, you peer *through* them, and seek the truth behind them. You look for the empowering factors, and disregard the weakening factors.

Fear snuffs out authenticity.

Authenticity is freedom from fear.

In fact, fear disconnects you from your greater self, and from the Universe at large, which is your source of insight, wisdom, and intuition. Allowing yourself to slip into the white water rapids of the fear stream is one of the quickest ways for your entire system to crush in on itself, pinching off anything but itself to sit inside a dark little box of nightmares.

This is a basis of what the Christian concept of "sin" is an illustration of. In that spiritual path, sin is disobedience to God, and a wall that instantly separates the seeker from the Almighty. Sin pinches off the connection to God, creating blockages. Fear pinches off the connection to the free-flowing and all-knowing energy of the Universe, which is the same energy you and all things are made of—you are made in the image of the Universe.

You can easily pinch yourself off by clinging too tightly to the desired or expected results of something. This is another subtle form of being attached to outcomes. If you place too great of an expectation on a specific result or goal, and things do not work out that way, you have set yourself up for disappointment, which can spiral out of control and easily invite negativity for some. The fear here creates worry that what you want will not come true. Both time and energy are wasted trying to force and twist things to be how you want, and anger then arises, if it continues to slip from your controlling grip.

This is not to say to hold low expectations for everything you do, simply to avoid disappointment. On the contrary, energy attracts more energy of the same frequency, so you *want* to aim high and dream big, or you'll never attain anything beyond the borders of your comfort zone.

Instead, the goal is to aspire for a mark, and maintain your integrity and authenticity, even if that mark is not met. Rather than surrender to the human ego's urges to sink and deflate at a so-called "failure," the Lightworker has the foresight and higher wisdom to understand that there is no such thing as failing — there is only doing. If the bulls-eye is missed by a couple inches to the left, the aim is simply adjusted a bit to the right, and the arrow is re-shot.

This fearless example of determination and commitment will reach a far wider audience than it ever would if you stood on a street corner with a megaphone shouting *"Never give up! Never surrender!"*

As a human, it is so very easy to freak out and nose-dive into the energy of despair when things are not going "right," and to be comfortably at ease when things *are* going well. This is another mirror of the unfortunate way it takes being affected personally in some way for many people to respond and take action on an issue.

As a Lightworker, your intention and example should be a clear and consistent mind, examining the details and true reality of a situation before reacting, ever seeking and focusing on the truth and grander scheme behind all things.

• 10 •
THE GAME

MANY LIGHTWORKERS ARE ALSO some form of intuitive reader or spiritual counselor. Often working within their own home or at metaphysical fairs and spirit expos, Lightworkers generally discover they are able to offer a variety of services such as tarot or oracle card readings, crystal work, past life readings, palm readings, and energy healings.

People sit down at their tables or booths, searching for answers to the unknown, and many of these people are regular returning clients.

What are they searching for the answers to?

A majority of the time, they are seeking peace of mind from their *fears*. They are seeking the easy way for a certain thing.

If something that is unknown—like the future—can become the known, and what is unexpected can become expected and made to show itself, then how much easier everything would be to plan for and navigate!

And how utterly boring that would be, if you really think about it — to constantly know everything that is going to happen, with no surprises whatsoever?

The human mind takes comfort in routine. Routines are safe, predictable, and simple.

But these things can never be known with absolute certainty. That is not how intuitive readings work, though many "Lightworkers" intentionally portray themselves and their work in this way.

All things in this Universe are made of energy; everything from solid objects to the thoughts in your head are pure energy. Intuitive readings are energy readings that feel into the zillions of possible pathways — the "threads" or "timelines" — any one thing could potentially go. Some readers can easily see and follow the karmic energy thread of the question asked by the client — the possible *effects* that may occur if the current *causes* continue in their present course — and then relay and translate this information to the client.

Yet even if a timeline thread can be pinned down with clarity in this here-and-now moment, it *still* does not mean that is absolutely what is going to happen. Every action, decision, and thought shifts and changes the timelines with every breath. The very fact of being told a certain timeline can alter the course of it instantly, rendering it no longer true, or a less likely possible outcome. Hundreds of time travel science fiction movies and books have explored the concept of timelines and alternate dimensions, and they all hold pieces of the truth.

The science of quantum mechanics explores the existence of alternate realities, which exist overlaying each other simultaneously. I feel there is essentially an alternate reality for each choice you make, and with each choice you make, you step across the threshold into an alternate timeline, as if you were switching lanes on the interstate highway.

This is also what "everyone is in their own world" and "being in your own little world" means. Every single person lives in and operates from their own world, created from their decisions, perceptions, and desires.

If definite outcomes cannot be accurately predicted until they actually manifest in your own little present world, then why do so many waste their time and energy trying to get a peek into the unknown?

Once someone believes this sort of thing is true and can be done, or gets a taste of it being real, it is extremely easy to become addicted to it, just as gambling or sex can be—there's always room and time for "just a little more."

This is the game many are sucked into.

Hollywood does not particularly help in these situations, as more and more movies and books on witches, fortune tellers, vampires, and psychics grow in popularity daily.

The fact that some people claim the Lightworker title for themselves, yet are no more than charlatans or even legitimate intuitive readers misusing their abilities to manipulate and control others, adds to the misrepresentation of those who do give their all to help and heal others from healthy motives.

Why do so many "Lightworkers" go the Hollywood way?

One reason could be they enjoy the attention and the sense of importance they get when people come to them for major issues and questions. Another reason may be they are hooked on the feeling of power they get at telling people whatever they want, and having the people believe and do whatever they say. They can grow arrogant and self-important, and often begin to truly believe they are all-knowing and have all the one true answers.

Being a true Lightworker requires an unshakable humility and humbleness, an understanding of how the energies work, and the strength to do or say whatever has to be done or said — or *not* done and said.

Discretion and discernment are extremely

important senses for the Lightworker to develop and stay constantly in tune with. There are some who argue that if an insight is "given" or "shown," it is to be told to the client, no matter what. Based on this argument, if someone asked how a clock worked, would it be better for them to hear how each cog and wheel fits into each specific place to cause something to happen, which causes something else to happen, and then something else, thus telling the time, or would an explanation as simple as *"The motor moves the hands around to show the time"* be sufficient?

You return to the point of speaking to others at whatever level they are currently at — not because they are stupid or dense, but simply because that is where they currently are in their journey.

If someone is told *"You may die if you get in your car today,"* how will that be taken? If they take it to heart, they may fly into a desperate panic, and hide under their blankets in bed all day, accomplishing nothing, including other things that may *need* to happen for the best of all involved. This would be disempowering them, and they may even refuse to drive ever again!

If that same person instead received their intuitive news in a more compassionate and discerning manner, such as *"Hmm... You might want to be extra alert to everything around you; be careful and aware — I see the possibility of a shift in events soon,"* then this would be empowering the client, and leaving the outcome solely in their responsibility, still calm and collected.

Yet discernment and intuition are major factors in reading. At times, there will be a very strong urging or prodding that the client *needs* to hear something in particular. It may be something the reader does not want to say or do, but in this case, *not* telling it may be the more harmful thing to the client in that moment rather than telling it.

Each case is different, and intuitive connection is a must.

There are many readers who tell the client whatever they think the client wants to hear, just as there are readers who intentionally tell the client whatever it is the reader wants them to hear for their own purposes. Unfortunately, things like *"I'm going to need to see you every week for the next year in order to clear you of this, and it will cost this much money each visit,"* or *"I'm sensing that you will be meeting your soul mate very soon, and in fact, it's me,"* are similar things I've heard from the mouths of "Lightworkers" many times.

This, too, breaks my Heart.

Extreme authenticity and integrity is clearly a major requirement for those who call themselves Lightworker, and the Lightworker can *never* do the work for the client. The clients are on their own journey, and only they can do their own work. Discernment is again key in determining when to quit giving your energy to a one-way effort—if they are not willing to do their own work, then you and the client are both wasting your time and energy.

In the same way clients can become "addicted" to the game of readings, the reader can also easily grow attached to consulting their tools before making any decision or taking any action, especially in the beginning. Rather than simply living their life day by day and making use of their intuitive abilities in the present moment of each thing that happens, they become dependent and disempowered, always having to pull out their pendulum in the grocery store to decide which brand to purchase, or do muscle testing divination to decide if they should walk the track at the park clockwise or counter-clockwise.

One of the first tools I learned to work with as I was discovering myself and finding my way on my journey was tarot cards. I became fixated with them, checking with the cards on every little thing.

Using them, applying them, and comparing them to what actually happened in the past, present, and future *did* help me learn to read them very well, and was actually an important self-counseling tool that got me through a rough period in my life, but I eventually realized I was relying on them *too* much, obsessively *over-*analyzing each reading, and reading *too* much into them, trying to divine exactly what it was saying or what was going to happen. I was losing both time and energy, and completely missing the present moment.

As I went to the cards less and less, and trusted myself and my own intuition more and more, I found it actually felt so much more empowering to feel and think for myself — and that I could attain the same results on my own.

For me, reading tarot started as something fascinating, then grew into a "cool" trick I found I was good at and could get attention from. From there, it evolved as I evolved, and became a tool for my intention to genuinely help others. Eventually I grew hesitant to read cards at all for that purpose, as I saw it enabling so many to shrug their responsibilities. I found that directing others to take up their own empowerment was much more effective for *all* involved.

Tools such as cards and pendulums are meant to be merely stepping stones — a sort of child's game to teach and practice greater skills. Like training wheels on a bicycle that eventually come off when you've learned to keep your balance, these things will eventually fade away from you, and you will wake up one day wondering exactly when you became a fully authentic Lightworker.

• 11 •
THE AUTHENTICITY

WHEN LIGHTWORKERS REACH A certain point of being overwhelmed by the "lower" energies surrounding them on a daily basis, it becomes even more apparent to them that they are not from this place. The knowledge that they are different than the majority of people on the planet at this time sort of slaps them in the face, reminding them they are aliens in a way — strangers in a strange land.

I feel this is largely the energy of Light they brought with them, the higher frequencies they operate from, which is a very different vibration than the energies of this time.

Lightworkers often carry memories or impressions of "Home" within them. They have an ingrained sense of somewhere they were before, and feel they are heading back to once again.

Then why did they come here in the first place, especially if their energy does not match the vibrations of this planet and dimension, and they are returning right back to the place they came from? Why did they not simply stay where they were? And even if they *do* make a difference while they are here, won't it all slip back into darkness, if the light is once again switched off?

How do they know it will "stick?"

They know the same way we know that dropping even a single drip of black paint into a mixture on an artist's palette will darken the entire shade of color once it is mixed in.

They know the same way a spinning top will careen out of control from the tiniest tap, losing its balance and shifting its motion in response to the bump — the cause and effect of its karma.

They know the same way two frequencies vibrating close to each other will naturally sync up and begin resonating in harmony.

Everything changes everything, and continues from there.

To go back into the dark after seeing and experiencing the light would be like trying to return to the days when candles were the only source of light for a home. Once electricity was discovered and harnessed to light the dark nights, that "luxury" was known and experienced. Now, even if electricity was wiped from existence, it would still be in your conscious awareness, and you would always strive to find a way to "rediscover" and make use of electricity once again. You will always seek the light.

When you are in the middle of a thing, it is so easy to stoop down to the level of that thing and begin to resonate with that vibration yourself. If you have decided and dedicated yourself to being a Lightworker, then "stepping down" and becoming fully like what is around you is not holding to your authenticity at all.

There is a huge difference between being *in* the world and being *of* the world, and this is the question that you as a Lightworker must check in with yourself and ask daily. Awareness of self is the most important key to being in any sort of position to help others. Your intentions and motives must be looked at in complete naked honesty at all times—has human ego crept in? Has the love of attention, power, or money snuck into your drive?

And if you dedicate to a certain course of action, or a specific way to present yourself, make that decision, then *do* it. So many often decide to be a Lightworker, spiritual counselor, or intuitive reader, then complain incessantly at the work it creates or the circumstances it brings about. Your actions will always speak louder than your words, and if you are only pretending to be a certain way, it will eventually be cracked wide open. You must have fully weighed and felt into the decision that this field of work is definitely what you want to do. A decision led by the Heart may be the only one strong enough to survive.

On the other side of this coin of experience, natural Lightworkers often find themselves hesitating to follow the "call" toward a specific "job," or even the work itself. Fears that they may not be able to accomplish what they set out to do, fears of what others will think or say or do if they commit to this work, and fears of not being or feeling in control of their own lives anymore pin them down and render them immobile.

And if they are feeling such a strong call from their Heart, then that is who they are at their core. Therefore, ignoring or denying that call is then their form of inauthentic living.

When you are not living authentically — whether ignoring your Heart, or posing as something you're not — it places a strain on your entire system, inviting an internal anxiety and stress at your cellular and energetic levels, which can easily cause a lack of patience and compassion. In this way, you can actually cause harm to others around you by not honoring your own authenticity, and not simply harm to yourself. Nothing you do ever affects only you. Everything is connected to everything.

The longer an imbalance like this is allowed to continue, the more likely it will be to begin showing up in your physical body as an illness or disease. This is not to say that all sickness and disease is caused from these levels or situations, but it is certainly a possibility, depending on whatever other conditions and factors are at play in your energy field.

I was the personal assistant of a quadriplegic man for a while, shuttling him to doctor appointments, running errands, answering emails and phone calls, and helping him with his exercises. This man had only recently become paralyzed, and had previously been a well-known dancer and dance teacher. His paralyzation set in extremely quickly and quite mysteriously — he had been to see specialist doctors all over the country, and not a one of them could determine what was wrong with him. There had been no accident or event of any kind that would cause such an effect. They were utterly baffled as his condition continued to deteriorate.

As I got to know him and talk with him, I learned that his ex-wife had left him for one of his dance students, and although they still had a friendly relationship from sharing a daughter together, he held a deep bitterness and resentment inside. That was *his* wife, and he loved her more than anything, even though she had betrayed him.

It was shortly after this event in his life that his condition began to set in. I realized that the energy and emotion he harbored and clung to had begun to shift his energy from the inside, eating away at him until it began to display visible signs in his physical body in the completely paralyzing form of no disease or brain damage any doctor had ever seen before or could identify. He simply began to shut down.

Unfortunately, he was never able to release and come to terms with the situation and himself. He eventually lost the battle and his life. I always wonder if he would have been able to fully recover if he had found a way to take up his own power and authenticity.

Knowing yourself well enough to say no to something when necessary, being true to who you know yourself to be despite the opinions and influences of those around you, avoiding or saying no to the things you recognize will cause you to feel guilty, hurt, or angry afterwards, and being boldly honest with yourself on every level are ways you are able to "keep an eye on yourself," empower yourself, and be in control of yourself. By taking full responsibility for yourself and all you think, say, and do, you are shining your Light as bright as possible.

Another inclination I've seen many Lightworkers struggle with is that of "hiding" their Light "for the sake of others." They feel the other person may be intimidated or feel inferior by their practiced ways, and so "dim" it down or play a role, thinking this will encourage and "boost" the other to feel better and do better.

This is *never* helpful.

Not only does this set your own empowerment and authenticity aside, it essentially enables the other person to continue in their complacent little comfort zone, never being pressed to grow beyond the borders of their box. This is encouraging them to be inauthentic themselves.

Playing a role such as this is not showing love at all, but actually damaging the other — how would removing a shining example benefit anything and cause any growth?

Ultimately, it would be sabotaging yourself as well, because if such inauthentic posing continues for long at all, you will find yourself feeling trapped, frustrated, bitter, and angry. To resolve it would require revealing your true self, which would expose that you've been deceitful, and would cause the other more confusion and harm than they ever would have experienced previously if they had merely had a model example to work towards — and that would have been work they accomplished themselves, in their own free will.

If you ever do find yourself swimming in emotions such as anger or frustration, you are able to turn within, check in with yourself once again, and begin questioning everything to trace the line backwards and pinpoint the root cause of the emotions. Sometimes you may find they are not your own emotions, but have been absorbed from others and the environment around you. Other times you may find they do originate with yourself, such as in the "playing a role" illustration.

For example, if it is anger you are experiencing, questions you may ask to narrow down the cause may be *"Why does this thing make me angry?" "Am I angry because something I was attached to happening did not happen?"* or *"Is there an old conditioning being poked I have not healed yet?"*

No matter what you pinpoint as you work with yourself, you *always* have the power to choose, decide, and do.

You always, *always* have the right and the responsibility to be as authentic as you possibly can, and this is the ultimate foundation and key to shining in this physical reality as a Lightworker.

I saw the way things were going,
a long time back.
I said nothing.
I'm one of the innocents who could have
spoken up and out
when no one would listen to the 'guilty.'
But I did not speak,
and thus became guilty myself…

—**Ray Bradbury,** *Fahrenheit 451*

ABOUT THE AUTHOR

I am Lloyd Matthew Thompson, and I've always been aware of energies my entire life — even while growing up in my strict religious family home of nine children, of which I was the oldest.

I've studied energy work in general since 2003, and energy healing specifically since 2007, attaining my Reiki Grand Master level with nationally known energy healer and shaman Phyllis Maxey.

I have been an intuitive reader since 2002, working local metaphysical and spirit fairs, offering energy healing, tarot card readings, and intuitive artwork readings, which combined my life-long artistic abilities with my intuitive "psychic" abilities.

Raised Christian, I have since explored, experienced, and been shaped by many other paths, including Buddhism, Shamanism,

Paganism, and New Age. Whether writing, painting, drawing, or teaching, reflections of all these can be found within each body of my work.

I have written for various metaphysical and holistic blogs and magazines, both locally and globally, and have created my publishing project, *Starfield Press*, (**www.StarfieldPress.com**) as a platform for both my works and the works of others, both fiction and nonfiction.

I am the author of *The Natural Healer's Guide*, as well as *The Healer: A Novel*.

My intention in all my work is to inspire and uplift, encouraging all toward self-empowerment and the highest, most authentic states possible.

Much Love to you all.

Lloyd Matthew Thompson
Oklahoma City, OK
www.StarfieldPress.com

Books by Lloyd Matthew Thompson

THE ENERGY OF GOD

WISE ONE: THE SONG OF MANJUSHRI

LIGHTWORKER:
A CALL TO AUTHENTICITY

ENERGYWORKER:
A CALL TO EMPOWERMENT

THE NATURAL HEALER'S GUIDE

THE HEALER: A NOVEL

ROOT: A NOVELLA

AURA: A SHORT STORY

STARFIELD

ENERGY WORKER

A CALL TO EMPOWERMENT

BESTSELLING AUTHOR OF *LIGHTWORKER*
LLOYD MATTHEW THOMPSON

Look for *Energyworker: A Call to Empowerment*
Only from **Starfield Press**!

"Enlightening, empowering...
5-Star information!"

THE
NATURAL
HEALER'S
GUIDE

BESTSELLING AUTHOR OF *LIGHTWORKER*
LLOYD MATTHEW THOMPSON

Look for *The Natural Healer's Guide*
Only from **Starfield Press**!